Bob Wishart

FRANCIS FRITH'S

TOWN & CITY

MEMORIES

BRAINTREE

DAVID POSSEE has had a life-long interest in the history
of Braintree and is secretary of the local History Society.
He is a regular speaker at local groups, a tutor with WEA
and leads historical tours of the town centre. From his
researches he has published books on the Essex and Suffolk
Silk Industry, life locally during the First World War, and
the development of seaside resorts with special emphasis on
Essex, as well as writing articles for magazines.

FRANCIS FRITH'S
TOWN & CITY
MEMORIES

BRAINTREE

DAVID POSSEE

FRANCIS FRITH'S
TOWN & CITY
MEMORIES

First published as Braintree, A Photographic History of your Town
in 2001 by Black Horse Books, an imprint of The Francis Frith Collection
Revised edition published in the United Kingdom in 2005 by
The Francis Frith Collection as Braintree, Town and City Memories
Limited Hardback Edition 2005 ISBN 1-84589-052-3
Paperback Edition 2005 ISBN 1-85937-987-7

British Library Cataloguing in Publication Data

Braintree
Town and City Memories
David Possee

The Francis Frith Collection®
Frith's Barn, Teffont,
Salisbury, Wiltshire SP3 5QP
Tel: +44 (0) 1722 716 376
Email: info@francisfrith.co.uk
www.francisfrith.co.uk

Aerial photographs reproduced under licence from Simmons Aerofilms Limited
Historical Ordnance Survey maps reproduced under licence from Homecheck.co.uk

Printed and bound in England

Front Cover: **BRAINTREE, HIGH STREET 1906** 55533t
The colour-tinting in this image is for illustrative purposes only,
and is not intended to be historically accurate

FRANCIS FRITH'S
TOWN & CITY
MEMORIES

CONTENTS

THE MAKING OF AN ARCHIVE

Francis Frith, Victorian founder of the world-famous photographic archive, was a devout Quaker and a highly successful Victorian businessman. By 1860 he was already a multi-millionaire, having established and sold a wholesale grocery business in Liverpool. He had also made a series of pioneering photographic journeys to the Nile region. The images he returned with were the talk of London. An eminent modern historian has likened their impact on the population of the time to that on our own generation of the first photographs taken on the surface of the moon.

Frith had a passion for landscape, and was as equally inspired by the countryside of Britain as he was by the desert regions of the Nile. He resolved to set out on a new career and to use his skills with a camera. He established a business in Reigate as a specialist publisher of topographical photographs.

Frith lived in an era of immense and sometimes violent change. For the poor in the early part of Victoria's reign work was a drudge and the hours long, and ordinary people had precious little free time. Most had not travelled far beyond the boundaries of their own town or village. Mass tourism was in its infancy during the 1860s, but during the next decade the railway network and the establishment of Bank Holidays and half-Saturdays gradually made it possible for the working man and his family to enjoy holidays and to see a little more of the world. With characteristic business acumen, Francis Frith foresaw that these new tourists would enjoy having souvenirs to commemorate their days out. He began selling photo-souvenirs of seaside resorts and beauty spots, which the Victorian public pasted into treasured family albums.

Frith's aim was to photograph every town and village in Britain. For the next thirty years he travelled the country by train and by pony and trap, producing fine photographs of seaside resorts and beauty spots that were keenly bought by millions of Victorians.

THE RISE OF FRITH & CO

Each photograph was taken with tourism in mind, the small team of Frith photographers concentrating on busy shopping streets, beaches, seafronts, picturesque lanes and villages. They also photographed buildings: the Victorian and Edwardian eras were times of huge building activity, and town halls, libraries, post offices, schools and technical colleges were springing up all over the country. They were invariably celebrated by a proud Victorian public, and photo souvenirs – visual records – published by F Frith & Co were sold in their hundreds of thousands. In addition, many new commercial buildings such as hotels, inns and pubs were photographed, often because their owners specifically commissioned Frith postcards or prints of them for re-sale or for publicity purposes.

In order to gain some understanding of the scale of Frith's business one only has to look at the catalogue issued by Frith & Co in 1886: it runs to some 670 pages. By 1890 Frith had created the greatest specialist photographic publishing company in the world, with over 2,000 stockists! The picture on the right shows the Frith & Co display board on the wall of the stockist at Ingleton in the Yorkshire Dales (left of window). Beautifully constructed with a mahogany frame and gilt inserts, it displayed a dozen scenes.

POSTCARD BONANZA

The ever-popular holiday postcard we know today took many years to appear, and F Frith & Co was in the vanguard of its development. Postcards became a hugely popular means of communication and sold in their millions. Frith's company took full advantage of this boom and soon became the major publisher of photographic view postcards.

Francis Frith died in 1898 at his villa in Cannes, his great project still growing. His sons Eustace and Cyril continued their father's monumental task, expanding the number of views offered to the public and recording more and more places in Britain, as the coasts and countryside were opened up to mass travel. The archive Frith created continued in business for another seventy years. By 1970 it contained over a third of a million pictures of 7,000 cities, towns and villages. The massive photographic record Frith has left to us stands as a living monument to a special and very remarkable man.

This book shows Braintree as it was photographed by this world-famous archive at various periods in its development over the past 150 years. Every photograph was taken for a specific commercial purpose, which explains why the selection may not show every aspect of the town landscape. However, the photographs, compiled from one of the world's most celebrated archives, provide an important and absorbing record of your town.

A BRIEF HISTORY OF THE TOWN

A frequently asked question is: how old is Braintree? In common with the majority of towns, it is difficult to pinpoint an exact date when Braintree came into being, and we have to rely on archaeological evidence. Such evidence suggests a date of about 1500 BC on two distinct sites: one is on the River Brain at the foot of Chapel Hill, and the other is somewhere in the vicinity of Bank Street on that east-west road.

In AD10 the Catuvellauni, under Cunobelin, marched through the area and established a new capital at Lexden called Camulodunum (Colchester). When the Romans invaded in AD43, Camulodunum was one of their first conquests. The Romans built a new settlement - Colonia Claudia Victricensis - but the Iceni led by Boudicca razed this to the ground in AD61.

With the rebuilding of Colonia came the military presence of a garrison. The old prehistoric road to the west was rebuilt, linking Colchester with St Albans, and settlements were built at approximately 7-mile intervals to service the military traffic. One of these, built sometime about AD100, was Braintree. Its importance was enhanced by the fact that in Braintree roads converged from Chelmsford, Cambridge, Rivenhall and Suffolk. There is archaeological evidence to suggest the existence of shops and an iron foundry in Braintree. The local farmers would have supplied food for people and provender for animals.

From the middle of the 5th century AD the Romans left Britain, and this part of the country became subject to invasion from the Saxons. In Braintree the Saxons made their main settlement on the south-facing slopes of the Brain Valley at Chapel Hill, with a smaller one around the crossroads.

The entries in the Domesday Book of 1086, after the Norman invasion, give an insight into Braintree at that time: Branchtreu (about 30 acres) was by the crossroads, and the larger settlement of Raines Magna (about 400 acres) was by the River Brain. By the mid 12th century, Braintree was on the important pilgrimage route

CHAPMAN AND ANDRE'S MAP 1777

Looking at a map of North Essex, it is clear to see the townships of Braintree and Bocking straddling the crossroads of important east-west and north-south routes. This gives a clue to why settlements grew up here. Although the road to Colchester is shown on Ordnance Survey maps as a Roman road, its existence as a route to the coast can be traced back 2,000 years before the Romans came.

to Bury St Edmunds and Walsingham. The Bishop of London, the then landowner, was granted a charter for a market and an annual fair in 1199. The result of this was the building of a new town around the crossroads.

From the 15th century, a flourishing woollen industry developed; this contributed to the wealth of the town for almost 400 years. As the 19th century dawned, Braintree was still very much a market town contained within the area of the medieval town. The woollen industry had ceased, and the silk industry had taken its place. The railway arrived in 1848, and was the catalyst for still further town development.

The entry on Braintree and Bocking from Whites 'Directory' of 1848 reads: 'Braintree, a well-built and improving market town, is partly in its own parish, and partly in that of Bocking, and extends about 2 miles on both sides of the high road southward from the river Pant, or Blackwater, to the small river Brain; 12 miles N by E of Chelmsford, 6 miles S by W of Halstead, 9 miles E of Dunmow and 40 miles NE of London. The northern part of the town, extending to the river Blackwater, is in Bocking parish, and the southern part in Braintree parish, but some streets in the heart of the town are in both parishes. The town rises boldly from both rivers, and the principal street is a great thoroughfare, and has many good houses, inns and well stocked shops, as also have some of the other streets. Braintree parish contained 3,670 inhabitants and Bocking, 3,437 in 1841. The town is being considerably improved on its south-eastern side, where a new road has been made, and a handsome station erected for the railway from Witham opened in 1848'.

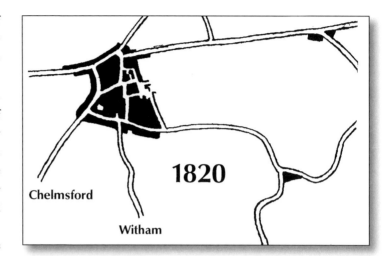

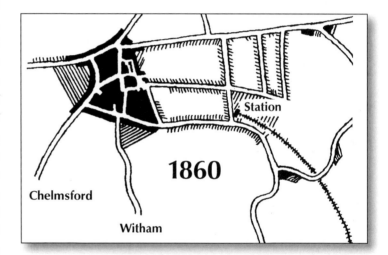

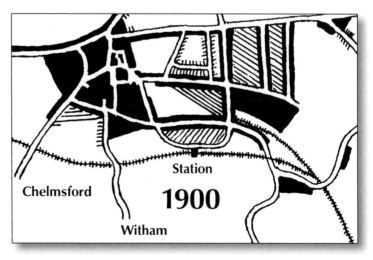

SKETCH MAPS OF TOWN DEVELOPMENT

HIGH STREET AND GREAT SQUARE

The High Street begins just after the junction of London Road and Pierrefitte Way, and it follows the line of the Roman road as far as Sandpit Lane. It is thought that the Roman road went straight on through the area of the present day George Yard shopping centre to Bank Street (which until the 1840s was a continuation of the High Street), but the present street is south of this alignment. At its eastern end, as it reaches Bank Street, it becomes Great Square. In the Sandpit Lane area it is a typical narrow medieval street, which gradually widens as it meets Bank Street. The oldest buildings on the southern side are from the 15th-16th century, whereas on the other side they date from the 17th century. This would possibly suggest that when the new market was set up, this side of the street was rebuilt.

By the 17th century this area in front of the Horn Hotel (55533, right) was being used as a meeting place for the weekly market and the annual fair. Cattle and horses were still being bought and sold in the High Street in the later years of the 19th century. It is also the setting for the famous 1826 market print of people attending Braintree Market. In 1979 the Chamber of Trade commissioned a painting, depicting members of the local community standing in the same place.

In 1890, local people owned the shops; but according to Kelly's Directory of 1906, the International Tea Co had opened a shop in the High Street. The Home & Colonial followed in 1910 joined by the Maypole in the 1930s. These national companies offered a wider range of groceries at cheaper prices, and provided competition to the local grocers.

H Cook the pork butcher's shop was in the High Street in 1902 (48277, page 14-15), and it was still there in 1923 (74832, page 16). Cooks were famous for their pork pies. Many a local supper consisted of a Cook's pie washed down with a pint of local ale. There is also a fruit and flower shop next door, which in 1923 was owned by Thomas Kirby. However, there is a new building to the right of Cook's with steps up to it and 'Restaurant' on the fascia. This is, in fact, the newly-built Central Cinema, which was built in 1922 by a local builder Mr F A Brown. By 1929, the cinema was owned and run by Shipman & King. The restaurant was a café that served light refreshments. By 1954, according to a projectionist who was there at that time, the tables and chairs were still in place

but not in use. The Picture Palace (later the Embassy) had already arrived in Fairfield Road; this shows the growing popularity of the cinema as entertainment. I am reliably informed that in the 1920s it cost 2d to go to the Saturday morning film show at the Central, but only 1d at the Palace. The Central Cinema closed in 1963 when watching television became more popular. Next door to the cinema, at 63/65 High Street, is Aldiss Brothers, who were drapers. By some quirk the Cinema was also 65 High Street!

HIGH STREET AND GREAT SQUARE

HIGH STREET 1906 55533

Two family firms with a long connection with the High Street were Townrows and Joscelynes. Charles Townrow started the business in 1871 in a rented shop at 65 High Street. The family, in common with most business families of the time, lived above the shop. As the business grew, a shop was purchased at 42 Bank Street and the family moved to the house adjoining the Great House in Great Square. In 1916, 51-53 High Street was purchased. Because of the war, opening was delayed until 1919. In 1954, 76/78 High Street, a shop once occupied by Joscelynes, was purchased. Finally in 1985 the Central Cinema premises were bought from Tesco, and a department store was created here and in the shop next door. The business is now run by the fourth generation of the family.

Various members of the Joscelyne family have run businesses in Braintree since 1777. No 62 High Street was bought in 1791 and was one of their business premises until 1981, when their furnishing shop was closed down. Kelly's Directory for 1855 shows

HIGH STREET AND GREAT SQUARE

that James Joscelyne was at No 78 High Street as a bookseller, stationer and printer, whereas John was an auctioneer and cabinet maker at No 62. By the early 20th century these businesses were run by the next generation, Charles and Henry Joscelyne. Henry was by this time an estate agent and furniture remover as well. In 1925, No 60 and 62 High Street were made into one shop; the present-day style of the building dates from this period. Then in 1957 No 64 and 66 High Street were purchased to become a china and glass department. The estate agents business moved in 1961 to new premises at 18-22 Bank Street, where the business continues today as Joscelyne Chase.

Among the significant buildings of the High Street is the Corn Exchange, the building with the clock (46241, left); it was built in 1839 to replace the Market Cross building in New Street, which had fallen into disrepair. This was the place which farmers visited on Market Day to sell their produce - wheat, barley, hay and straw - to the merchants, who had stands in the exchange. Whilst the farmers were doing business, their wives visited the shops. In more recent times part of the building became the premises of Nicholls Bros, suppliers of radios, televisions and record players. Many people remember the Corn Exchange as the place for roller-skating and dances. Unfortunately it was demolished in the 1970s.

HIGH STREET 1900 46241

This street scene has some interesting features. For instance, outside the Corn Exchange, behind the boy with a bicycle, is a coachman wearing a top hat. Compare this with the photos of 1960 and 1965 that show motorcars and bicycles. The building on the left with the chimneystack of four pots was built in 1896 as the Post Office. The façade contains decorative brickwork, the date 1896 and the initials GTB, which were the initials of George Thomas Bartram who had the building erected. Before that time the Post Office was in one of the shops in the High Street. In 1935 the Post Office moved to new premises in Fairfield Road, and the building in the High Street became the town's Labour Exchange.

BRAINTREE

HIGH STREET 1902 48277

Another significant building was the Horn Hotel. This was one of the important inns of the town, dating back to at least the 17th century. We can clearly see the archway through which the coaches passed in 46241, page 12-13. Pigot's Directory of 1824 stated that the 'Norwich Day' coach called at the Horn at 10.00am and 4.00pm (at this time London was at least a 5-hour journey).

The Horn was also a meeting place for people attending the market, supplying not only drinks but meals. It continued to serve the community until 1970; it was then closed, and shops were put in either side of the carriageway, which still retains its cobbled entrance.

High Street and Great Square

Above Right: HIGH STREET c1960 B178033A

The Bank Street/Great Square corner was rebuilt in the 1930s with a building capped by a stylish cupola (centre, at the end of the street). Foster Brothers Ltd occupied the ground floor; although the official name of the property is London House, it became known as 'Foster's Corner'. The Pearl Assurance Co and Denis Keen, the optician, used the majority of the first floor. In 1959 Foster's moved to new premises in Great Square, and the building became the Braintree branch of the Midland Bank.

Right: HIGH STREET 1923 74832

HIGH STREET AND GREAT SQUARE

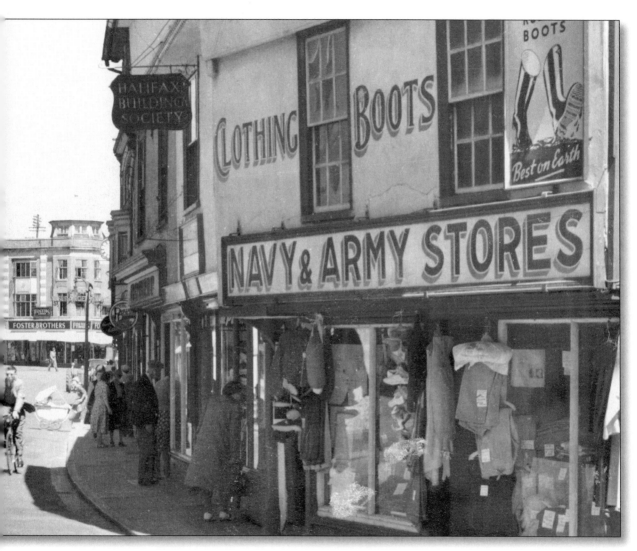

HIGH STREET c1965 B178043

In this photo you will notice that the cinema building was at this time a Tesco supermarket. The first self-service supermarket to open in Braintree in 1951 was Fine Fare, two doors away, which traded then as Elmos. It is believed that Elmos came to Braintree in about 1939. Fine Fare closed down in 1977. On the left is the Peter Townrow's ladies' wear shop, then part of the well-known family business.

GREAT SQUARE c1960 B178018

The road off to the right is New Street, where in 1620 the new market area was established. The large building
at the end of Great Square was known as the Great House. Its 18th-century brick façade hides a much earlier 15th-
century timber-framed house. In the 17th century it was the home of Benjamin Allen, a close friend of the famous naturalist John
Ray. Towards the end of the 19th century the ground floor was converted into a showroom for Albert Spearman, the cycle dealer.
In 1913 the Constitutional Club acquired the premises as their meeting place, although part of the ground floor has been used for
businesses ever since. At the time of the photograph these were Mrs Easlea's coffee bar and Mr Bocking's electrical shop.

MARKET PLACE AND MANOR STREET

MARKET SQUARE 1900 46244

GOSLING'S ENTIRE

H SANDERS

TRIBBLE HARNESS MAKER

The weekly market began with the granting of the charter in 1199, and has occupied many different sites in 800 years. The oldest building in the Market Place is the Bull Inn, dating back to the 17th century. In 1555, the Protestant martyr, William Pygott, was burned at the stake in the southern part of this area. This would suggest that this open space may have been in use for the market and fairs at this time; it was certainly conveniently far enough away from the buildings to prevent a fire from setting them alight.

Mr Cunnington's sketch plan of the Market Square above right, drawn from memory in 1840, shows the market place complete with the buildings and farmyard of Hyde Farm, also known as Manor Farm. The farm and adjacent properties were sold in 1847. Also to be seen are two inns, the Crown and Anchor and the Bull, serving the needs of those attending the market. The present day Market

Street was then known as Workhouse Lane, as the workhouse was situated in Workhouse Yard until 1837. The Union Workhouse opened in that year in Rayne Road to serve the Braintree area. The Market Street buildings, however, remained in use until they were demolished in 1970s, together with the Crown and Anchor and other buildings, to build a supermarket for Tesco.

Sixty years after Mr Cunnington's plan, Market Square had changed (see 46244, above). By 1900 it was known as the Cattle Market. The Nag's Head (right) was built on the site of the Hyde farmhouse sometime in the 1860s, replacing the Globe beerhouse that had started here in 1849. Opposite are the premises of H (Henry) Sanders, tinplate worker, otherwise known as a whitesmith. According to a directory for 1823, John Possell was a whitesmith here, followed by Charles Sanders, the father of Henry, in 1855. George Courtauld MP gave the fountain in the foreground in

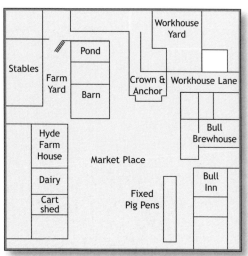

Causeway House premises in Bocking End.

The foundation stone was laid by Mr G T Bartram on 16 October 1926, and the building was officially opened by the Rt Hon the Earl of Crawford and Balcarres PC, KT on 22 May 1928. The cost, entirely borne by Mr William Julien Courtauld, was in excess of £50,000. The foundations, floors and roof are of reinforced concrete, and this makes the building an early example of the use of this material in buildings. The building is faced with narrow sand-faced bricks from Holland with a band of Portland stone at first floor and eaves level. On the front band are two coats of arms with the dates 1865 and 1913 carved in the stone: 1865 was when Mr Courtauld's mother married, and 1913 when Mr Courtauld married. The tower houses 4 quarter bells and 1 hour bell, as well as a four-faced clock with Westminster chimes. The hour bell is named Constance Cecily after William Julien's wife, who apparently cast silver coins into the furnace producing the metal for the bells. The Braintree coat of arms is emblazoned on the stonework beneath the bell tower. The tower is topped with a gilded figure of Truth: the Courtauld family motto is 'Tiens a la verité' (Hold to the truth), the English version of which became the motto for the Braintree coat of arms. The architect was Vincent Harris OBE, and the main contractors were E A Roome of London.

The portico with balcony above leads into the entrance lobby, from where stairs lead up to the Council Chamber and committee rooms. The columns on either side of the stairs contain carved roundels, one representing farming and the other industry. On the mezzanine

1882. It served the dual purpose of providing drinking water to both men and animals attending the market. The inscription reads: 'He sendeth the springs into the valleys which run among the hills. That ye may drink, both ye and your cattle and your beasts'.

Another 60 years on (see B178016, page 22-23), Market Square has changed very little in appearance, except that the troughs on the fountain are now full of geraniums rather than water. Tribble's saddler's shop is now Lingard's fabric shop, and garden area at the top of the square now has an infill of modern buildings. In the distance we can see the premises of Richardson & Preece, corn merchants, which is actually in Great Square. In 1900 it was the business of John Woodhouse, who was also a corn merchant.

The Town Hall (see B178003, page 25) is one of the town's most photographed buildings. It housed the council offices from 1928 until 1981, when the Braintree District Council built the new

Market Place and Manor Street

landing, the stairs go left and right to the upper floor. At this point, which is the back wall, there is a tall stained glass window depicting the Braintree coat of arms on a banner held by the female figure of Truth, with a view of St Michael's Church beneath. Within the stained glass is a coffee pot, the mark of the artist George Kruger Gray. In the vaulted ceiling in front of this window is a decorative painting of the Braintree and Essex coats of arms.

The ceiling of the Council Chamber has 14 decorative frescoes, depicting important events in the town's history, painted by Maurice Grieffenhagen RA, and on the ceiling in the Chairman's room is a decorative map of Essex by Henry Rusbury RA. Another interesting feature is the fact that all the rooms, even those used by the council officers, are wood-panelled. The Council Chamber is panelled in oak with an inlay of holly, the Chairman's room in walnut, and the committee rooms in pear wood. Downstairs, the rooms are panelled in oak, elm, chestnut and Australian beanwood.

View B178015 (pages 26-27) looks south, and shows the Nag's Head on one side and the Crown and Anchor opposite. The small white building to the left was at that time the office of the auctioneers Balls & Balls, who dealt with the sales at the weekly market. Set back, behind the two trees, is a Dutch-style building with bay windows. This was built in 1929 by W J Courtauld as the Corner House Restaurant as part of his plan to create a civic square.

Next door to the Town Hall is a small brick building, which is one of the market gatehouses shown in 50560 on page 24); they were moved and rebuilt with the building of the Town Hall. The gateway between the two is now the entrance to the new Braintree Library, which opened in 1996, and the plaque recording the opening of the Cattle Market can still be seen.

In between the Town Hall and the Corner House, the building with the rows of windows is the Post Office and Telephone Exchange, built in 1931 to replace the one in the High Street. This building was faced with bricks to match those of the Town Hall. It was moved into the Co-op premises in George Yard in the 1990s.

MARKET SQUARE c1960 B178016

Market Place and Manor Street

MARKET PLACE AND MANOR STREET

Opposite Top: MARKET PLACE 1900 46244x

This close-up shows the Bull Inn, which at this time was owned by the local brewer Oliver Gosling, hence the very large advertisement at roof level. Next door is the business of Tribble the harness maker, a reminder of the importance of the horse on the farm and as a means of transport. Robert Tribble took over an existing business in the 1880s and had moved to this site by 1899, according to Kelly's Directory. As motor vehicles took over the work of the horse, this trade diminished; by 1933 this building was Percy Haynes' refreshment rooms.

Opposite Bottom: MARKET PLACE 1903 50560

We are looking eastwards along Manor Street. The three-storey building to the left is the Nag's Head Inn, and buildings with the finial on top are the Manor Street School. The area with railings and the two low buildings is the site of the new cattle market, which was opened by George Courtauld on 1 October 1902, in time for the October Fair. It was on this site that the Town Hall was built in the 1920s. The open space beyond is the Fair Field, which was used for the two annual fairs. During the First World War it was in use as a field kitchen, baking bread for the troops billeted in the town. Manor Street was developed from 1847 to provide a link road from the centre of town to the new railway station, which was situated on a new road - Railway Street; the railway line to Witham opened in 1848. In the far distance is Manor Works, the factory of the Crittall Manufacturing Company.

Below: MANOR STREET AND THE TOWN HALL c1955 B178003

Market Place and Manor Street

Market Square c1955 B178015

ESSEX COUNTY MAP

Elmdon
Wendon Lofts
Littlebury
SAFFRON WALDEN
Steeple Bumpstead
Birdbrook
Ridgwell
Tilbury
Lit.
Stamborne
Great Yeldham
Hempstead
Wendens Ambo
Wimbish
Radwinter
Toppesfield
Castle Hedingham
Wicken Bonant
Newport
Thunderley
Great Sampford
Sible Hedingham
Rickling
Debden
Little Sampford
Finchingfield
Widdington
Little Bardfield
Blackwater
Weathersfield
Berdon
Quendon
THAXTED
Great Bardfield
Gosfield
Henham on the Hill
Ugley
Chickney
Shalford
River
Pledgen
Broxted
Lindsell
Bardfield Saling
Bentfield
Tilty
Great Easton
Great Saling
Boking
Elsenham
Panfield
Stansted Mounttitchet
Little Easton
Stebbing
Great Saling
Rayne
BRAINTREE
Birchanger
Takeley
Churchend
DUNMOW
Lit. Canfield
Br.
ORD
Great Hallingbury
Lit. Dunmow
Feelstead
Black Notley
Brain Riv.
Little Hallingbury
Barnston
Chatley
White Notley
Hatfield Broad Oak
Great Canfield
High Roothing
Lit. Leighs
Fairsted
Faulkbou
Aythorpe Roothing
High Easter
Gr. Leighs
Terling
Sheering
White Roothing
Barwick
Leaden Roothing
Pleshey
Gr. Waltham
WIT
Matching
Margaret Roothing
Good Easter
Mashbury
Lit. Waltham
Riv. Ter
Harlow
Abbots Roothing
Chignall Smealy
Broomfield
Latton
Berners Roothing
Chignall St. James
Boreham
H Pe
etswell
Little Laver
Beauchamp Roothing
Roxwell
Middle Mead
Laver Magdalen
High Laver
Shellow Bowels
Springfield
Lit. Baddow
Moreton
Fyfield
Willingale Doe
Willingale Spain
Writtle
Moulsham
Woodha Walt
Bobbingworth
Shelley
Norton Mandeville
Widford
CHELMSFORD
N. Weald Bassett
High Ongar
Great Baddow
Sandon
Danbu
Greenstead
CHIPPING ONGAR

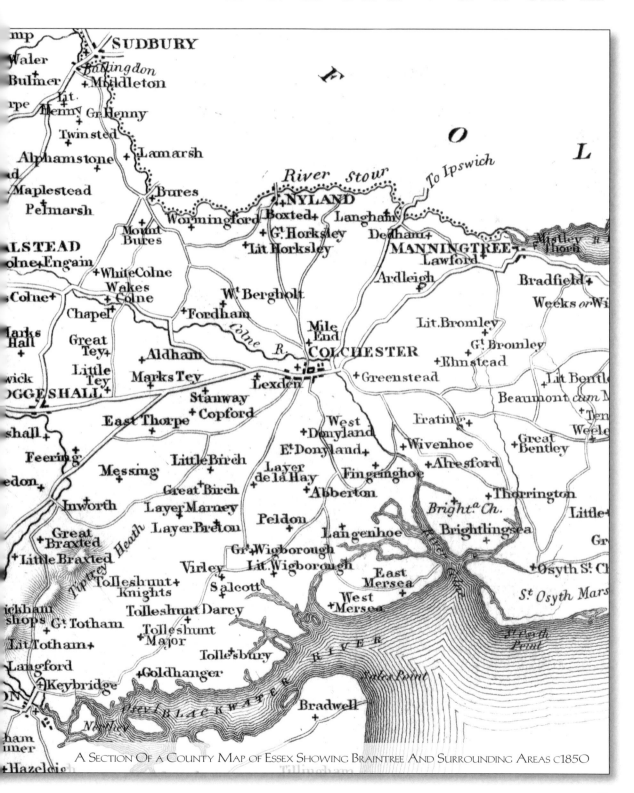

BANK STREET AND BOCKING END

The other main street is Bank Street, and visitors need to retrace their steps back into Great Square and then walk up Leather Lane, which opens out into Little Square. Here there are two examples of buildings dating back to the 15th century. Facing us as we come out of the square is the Swan.

The Swan Inn, an impressive 16th-century building built on the corner of Bank Street and Swanside (B178017) appears to be made up of three distinct parts. There is the main building on the corner plot, a lower range of buildings alongside and a gatehouse; the majority of the timberwork is original. A close study reveals small mullioned windows, doorways and near to the Bank Street corner what appears to be a shop front. Over the gateway are initials with a date of 1590. It may be that parts of the structure are much older than this, because this building is adjacent to Braintree's 13th-century market place in the area of Little Square.

By the Bank, Bank Street meets with Rayne Road and Coggeshall Road, which form the boundary with the neighbouring township of Bocking. John Bunyan, who visited the town in the 1670s, is thought to have preached in the area outside the White Hart. This part of Bocking, known as Bocking End, grew up with the new medieval town of Braintree. From its junction with the High Street the street is narrow. Many of the buildings date back to the 14th century, although their façades have been considerably modified over the years. Remnants of the original thatched roofs have been found in buildings in the lower end of the street.

In the 19th and early 20th century, people lived in the town centre. Many of them would have lived over their business premises. B178038 (page 34) shows the premises of FW Woolworth, who established their store in Bank Street in 1929 on the site of the house of one of Braintree's famous characters - Dr Jack Harrison (1857-1929). His family lived at the Great House in Great Square. Jack trained as a doctor, and set up his home and surgery in Bank Street. One of his claims to fame was the fact that when the telephone came to Braintree his number was Braintree 1. He served as the town's GP, and although health care had to be paid for he invariably tore up the bills for those patients who couldn't afford to pay. Behind the island buildings (see 50562, page 34) he had a garden, and on one occasion had a celebratory bonfire there for a friend whose wife had given birth to the first baby girl in the family for a generation!

Bank Street and Bocking End

Swanside c1955 B178017

Bank Street and Bocking End

BANK STREET c1965 B178038

In 1903 (50561, page 34-35) people walked or cycled, and if they were more affluent they used a pony and trap, governess cart or even a carriage. Sixty years on the motorcar is much in evidence, as well as a Lambretta scooter parked outside Stead & Simpson.

BANK STREET AND BOCKING END

BANK STREET 1903 50561

Bank Street was an extension of the High Street. Following the building of the new Braintree Bank in 1841, the street was renamed. The building next to Alden's was the Telephone Exchange, hence the sign 'Public Telephone Call Office'. It later moved to the Post Office in High Street.

Bank Street and Bocking End

Above:
BANK STREET 1903 50562

Bank Street and Bocking End

Bank Street c1965 B178041

Bank Street and Bocking End

BANK STREET AND BOCKING END

1920S ADVERTISEMENT FOR YE OLDE WHITE HART

THE WHITE HART c1960 B178039

Another notable Braintree citizen was Francis Henry Crittall. The glass-fronted shop, the third shop down from Woolworth's in B178038 (page 34), is that of Crittall & Winterton, the first name of which is very important in the life of Braintree. It was here that Francis Henry Crittall, founder of the Crittall Manufacturing Company, was born in 1860. The original building was destroyed by fire and replaced by the building shown in the photograph. In 1883, in a workshop behind the shop in George Yard, he started the manufacture of metal windows. Fortunately, this building has been preserved in the new development; it carries a commemorative plaque. The black crane used dates from 1883, and the building contains an original 19th-century Crittall metal

window. As the business expanded, a new factory was built in 1896 in Manor Street, which was known as the Manor Works. The firm went on to become internationally famous. The Manor Works site has now been replaced with a housing development, and Crittalls now occupy a site on the Springwood Industrial Estate, Rayne Road.

Photographs 50562 (page 35) and B178041 (pages 36-37) were taken 60 years apart: at once one is struck by just how much the street has changed over that period. In the middle distance in 50562 there is an island of shops. These were demolished, together with Dr Harrison's garden, in 1938 as a means of improving the traffic flow. The problem was not entirely solved, as the southern end of the

BANK STREET AND BOCKING END

street still retained its medieval street width. Whilst nowadays the whole street is known as Bank Street, the narrow street to the left of the island was then known as Swan Street. In 1941 bombs destroyed the corner, which was occupied by Blomfield's in 1903, together with two other shops along Bank Street. One of these premises was the branch of Lloyds Bank that had come to the town in the 1920s.

It was not until 1958 that the area was rebuilt with a sweep of rather unimaginative modern buildings, which lacked the character and individuality of those destroyed. In this new development there are just two shops - Dewhurst's and F Cloughton Ltd, the greengrocers and florists, who had moved from their Great Square premises when they were bought for re-development. Next door

to Cloughton's shop is a branch of the National Provincial Bank, which opened here in 1961. This closed with the merger with the National Westminster Bank, and the business transferred to that bank's premises in the High Street. This illustrates another change in town centres today: there tend to be many more service-type outlets. Next to the bank is 18/22 Bank Street, occupied by Joscelyne & Sons, auctioneers and estate agents.

The White Hart (see B178039, above) has suffered several changes in appearance during its lifetime. As a result, what we see disguises the true nature of the building(s) underneath. For instance, the façade in 1903 (50562, page 35, near left) is more accurate than the false black timbers we see in B178039. It may well have been the

BANK STREET AND BOCKING END

site of a mansio in Roman times; what we do know for certain is that the earliest part of the present structure is an aisled hall house from the 14th century. At that time it was a residence; it is thought to have developed as an inn in the late 16th century. With the advent of coach services through the town, it became an important coaching inn. Pigot's Directory of 1839 advertised coaches: 'From the White Hart - To London from Sudbury every forenoon at eleven, from Bury every afternoon at one and the 'Phenomena' from Norwich every afternoon at three'.

These services ceased with the arrival of the railway in 1848. However, a coach from the inn met each train at the station. From the 1920s advertisement, page 38, when the inn was known as 'Ye Olde White Harte Hotel', we see that buses had replaced the horse-drawn coaches going to the station. The building was used for meetings and events, the same kind of events that would be held in a public hall today. By the 1820s, the place was full to overflowing at times, and so in 1830 an Assembly Room was built at the rear of the building running alongside Coggeshall Rd.

BANK STREET AND BOCKING END

BANK STREET 1903 50562 DETAIL

This imposing neo-classical building on the corner of Bank Street and Rayne Road was built in 1840 for the local Sparrows Bank. The bank opened in the town on 2 September 1801. George Sparrow, one of the partners, lived in the nearby village of Gosfield. Until it was remodelled in the 1960s, the banking hall still retained its dark wood-panelled walls and counter, so reminiscent of Victorian banks. It merged, together with several other banks in the eastern counties, with Barclays of London in 1896 to form Barclays Bank Ltd. Today it is still the local branch of that bank.

BOCKING END c1955 B178032

The Co-operative's elegant range of buildings with a clock tower was another victim of 1960s development in the town. The Society was formed by a group of silk workers in 1864. The first shop was in a house in South Street, and then new premises were found in Swan Street, to the left of the island site. As business grew, it moved in 1875 to this site in Bocking End. The photograph shows the rebuilt premises of 1907. The resplendent clock tower was a landmark feature of the townscape. The Society merged with the Chelmsford Star Co-op, and now occupies a prestigious site in the George Yard shopping centre.

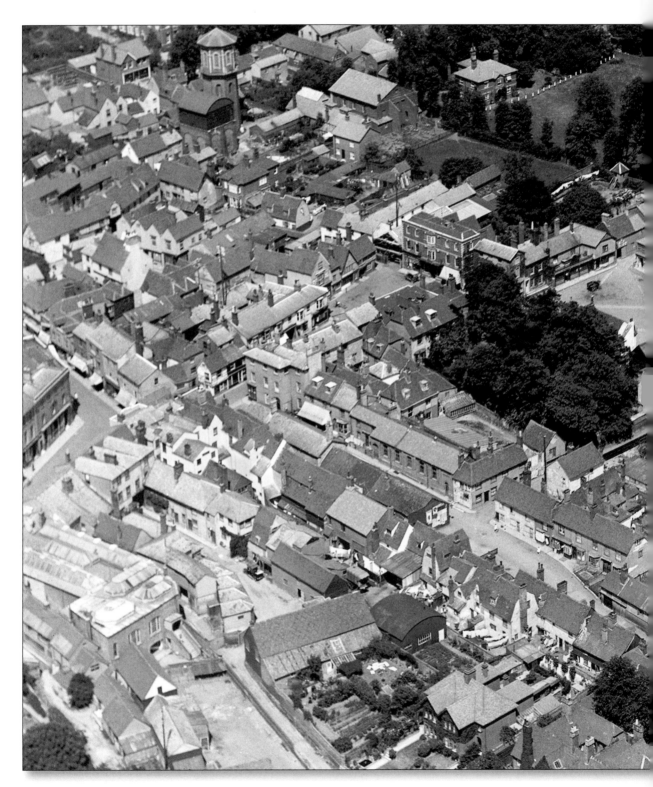

Braintree from the Air 1920 AF1743

Churches and Schools

CHURCHES AND SCHOOLS

Left: THE CHURCH 1900 46245

The spire of the parish church of St Michael is one of those landmarks that can be seen on the horizon as the traveller comes to the town by road. This, however, was not the original parish church. That was built in the Saxon settlement of Raines Magna, on the hillside overlooking the River Brain about one mile to the east of the present church. The building of St Michael's began sometime after the granting of the Market Charter in 1199. The original church became a chapel of ease, and not much is known about its use. Parts of the building still remained, in ruins, up until the middle of the 19th century. In 1905 the site was developed as the new foundry and factory of Lake & Elliot Ltd.

Bottom Left: RAYNE ROAD 1900 46243

Bottom Right: BRAINTREE, LONDON ROAD 1901 46721

The large building on the right was the Congregational Church at the time of the photograph; it is now known as Christchurch. This church was built in 1832 as a replacement for a chapel built originally in 1788 in Rayne Road. The new chapel could seat 900 people, and cost £1,400. It is faced with locally-made Braintree bricks. In 1866, schoolrooms and a hall were erected at the rear of the church.

The church that we see today is very different from that which was there in the early part of the 13th century. Although much altered, particularly in the mid 19th century, the structure is built of flint and rubble, interspersed with Roman brickwork that may well have been found when the foundations of the site were being prepared. The first building, in all probability, was rectangular, and consisted of a nave and chancel. The base of the present east wall of the chancel is the only surviving remnant of that early church; it contains quite a lot of Roman bricks. In 1240 the church was enlarged, with the addition of an aisle on the north side and a tower. In about 1350 the fine broach-spire was added. This terminates in a gilded weathercock - at that point it is 37 metres above the ground. Much of the original timberwork of the spire is in place today. At about the same time, a clerestory was added to the church, increasing the height of the nave and giving additional light to the building. This clerestory was replaced in about 1534, and was remodelled in the 1864 restoration. Prior to this, in 1526, the north aisle was enlarged, and a south

aisle was added in 1534. At the end of the north aisle a chantry chapel for the Jesus Guild was built in 1535. Wool merchants probably funded these major works in the 16th century.

By the early 19th century, the church was in a bad state of disrepair; the churchwardens tried to impose a compulsory rate on the townspeople to pay for repairs. Local non-conformists did not agree, and the matter was taken through the courts, eventually reaching the House of Lords. The Lords decreed that such a rate could not be compulsory. However, the money was raised voluntarily, and in 1864 work started on restoration - almost 30 years after the original rate demand was made. By this time, if it rained during a service, the parishioners had to put up umbrellas to keep dry! Much of the fabric of the old church was lost in the restoration, including the 16th-century clerestory, but nevertheless it is still an interesting place to explore. The original six bells were replaced in 1858, with an additional two added in 1899 and finally augmented to 10 in 1972.

Mention has already been made of William Pygott, burned at the stake for his faith in 1555; even before that time, Braintree

CHURCHES AND SCHOOLS

and Bocking were centres of non-conformity. It is recorded
that dissenters, as they were called, were meeting in Bocking in
the 1530s 'at William Beckwyth's house', and local Baptist and
Independent chapels claim their early beginnings with groups
such as these. In 1899, the following non-conformist churches
were meeting in the town: Quakers, Baptist, Strict Baptist,
Congregational, Primitive Methodist, Wesleyan, Salvation Army
and Unitarian. For a short period in the late 19th century, there
was a Free Church of England church.

View 46243, page 44, shows the Methodist Church at the corner
of Rayne Road and Sandpit Lane. This building was demolished in
1988-89 to make way for the George Yard shopping centre. The
exact date when Methodists first met in Braintree and Bocking is
unknown, although diocesan records for 1758 mention Methodists
worshipping in private homes. The congregation probably met in
a barn in Bradford Street, Bocking. John Wesley records a visit to
Bocking in his journal for October 1763.

This church in Rayne Road was opened on 9 July 1868, the
site having been purchased from George Vavasseur, a local silk
manufacturer. It was built in Gothic style, with red bricks and
Caen stone dressings, complete with a tower and spire at the north-
west angle. It could seat 320 downstairs, plus 120 in the gallery.
In 1936 part of the site was sold to the Braintree Co-operative
Society for new shops. The proceeds of this sale enabled a hall to
be built in Sandpit Lane, which was named the Wiseman Hall after
a former minister. In 1987 the church joined with the URC church
in London Road to become Christchurch.

In the 17th century, Braintree Grammar School was based in
the parish church. John Ray, the famous botanist, attended this
school before going to university. In the early part of the 19th
century, the Rev Scalé, Vicar of Braintree, opened a school. By
1820 another school had been opened in Manor Street under the
auspices of the Baptist Church. Kelly's Directory for 1855 also
mentions the following private schools: Miss Sarah Birdseye - Day
School in Sandpit Lane; Miss Louisa Cousins - Ladies' School in
London Road; Miss Catherine Hart - Ladies' Boarding School in
London Road.

The house to the left of the Congregational Church (46721, page
44) was Blandford House School in 1901. A Miss B Steel Johnson
ran this as a girls' day and boarding school. First mentioned in

CHURCHES AND SCHOOLS

THE PARISH CHURCH OF ST MICHAEL c1965 B178045

Churches and Schools

Above: THE COUNTY HIGH SCHOOL 1907 57571

Right: THE MANOR STREET SCHOOLS 1902 48284

The Baptist School, already mentioned, stood on part of this Manor Street site, which was purchased in 1862 with money left by George Courtauld. It became a Board School in 1875; according to the 1899 directory it had provision for 800 children, but the average attendance was 435. The school closed in 1990, and in 1994 the premises became the Braintree District Museum, which is a good place to go to find out more about the history of the area.

CHURCHES AND SCHOOLS

Up until the 1950s, Braintree College had its facilities scattered on several sites around the town. The site in Church Lane, Bocking was purchased in 1955 so that all departments could be on one site. The building is a typical design of the late 1950s, using glazed wall panels and concrete.

Kelly's 1899 directory, it seems to have closed some time after 1914. On the opposite side of the road, behind a pine tree, we can see a gable end. This is College House, where Mr Alexander Hart had his Classical, Mathematical and Commercial Academy in 1855. The academy continued under different people until the mid 1880s; one of its pupils was Francis Henry Crittall, who founded the window business.

The County High School (57571, left) was opened in 1906; it was provided by the Essex County Council at a cost of £10,000 to provide secondary education on land given by Mrs Sydney Courtauld of Bocking Place. According to the records for 1908, there were 126 pupils at the school. Initially it cost £2 2s per term, and was open for both boys and girls of 12 years of age and upwards, provided they passed the entrance examination. The architectural style is in the standard form for all High Schools provided throughout Essex at this time. The tower in later years housed a revolving ventilator. The school was merged with the Margaret Tabor School in the 1970s to become the Tabor High School. With the provision of new buildings in Panfield Lane in 1992, this building was vacated; it is now the local Social Services office.

Adult education began in the town in 1845 when a Mechanics' Institute was established in Rayne Road. George Courtauld provided a new building in Bocking End, which was known as the Braintree and Bocking Literary & Mechanics' Institution. Then in 1934 the Braintree Evening Institute was formed. Classes were held at the Braintree County High School outside normal school hours, using teachers from the school. With the outbreak of war in 1939 the Institute closed, but it re-opened in 1942 with the specific aim of training industrial apprentices. Classes were held on many different sites across the town. After the war it became the Technical and Arts Institute. By the 1960s all the teaching facilities were on the site at Church Lane, by which time it had become the College of Further Education. Finally, in 1991 it became Braintree College - a tertiary college for pupils aged 16 and over.

The Silk Mills 1902 48283

In 1810 George and Samuel Courtauld built this lath and plaster mill, seen here to the right of the chimney. This was built for Remington, Wilson & Co of Spitalfields at the foot of Chapel Hill. It was the first silk mill in the town, and was bought by Samuel Courtauld & Co in 1843. The brick silk mill alongside was built in 1859; it was destroyed by fire in 1909, but was replaced with a new building in 1910. The site today is a housing development.

SOUTH STREET 1909 62116

With the introduction of the silk industry in 1810, followed by the arrival of the railway in 1848, the town increased in size. Housing and industrial development grew up away from the town centre. The census returns for the 100 years from 1831 show not only the growth in population, but also the growth in the working population.

In South Street, houses were built that were typical of those that were built in Braintree from the 1890s to house the increasing number of people coming into the town to work. In photograph 62116, above, a view looking away from the town, the houses near the telegraph post have decorative brick tiles in panels between the windows. Both these and the bricks would have been made in local brickfields. At one time there was a brick works behind the houses on the right. Note the wall postbox, once quite a common feature in our towns. According to Kelly's Directory, post was collected from this particular box at 7.50am, 10.30am, 3.40pm and 7.35pm on weekdays. Quite prominent in the distance is the gable end of a large building. This is the Braintree Brewery in Railway Street, founded in about 1868 and owned in 1909 by Ernest Ingold. The brewery closed in 1939, and the site was re-developed for housing in 2001.

If we turn right by the post box in 62116, we come to Station Road, now known as Station Approach (57567, page 53). When the

A GROWING TOWN

Above: SOUTH STREET 1909 62117
The large weather-boarded buildings on the left are the silk mills of Warner & Sons, who had taken over the business of Walters & Co in 1894. Daniel Walters came to the town in 1822, and these mills were built in 1856. Behind these is another range of buildings constructed in 1869. Both firms produced silk products for the royal family, and Warners have woven velvet for every coronation since that of Edward VII.

Left: THE AVENUE 1906 55538

A Growing Town

Station Road 1907 57567

THE AVENUE 1901 46722

This photograph and 55528 (page 52) give a good idea of the type of houses that were provided in the Avenue; these were larger houses, suitable for members of the professional classes.

A GROWING TOWN

railway line was extended from Braintree to Bishop's Stortford in 1869, a new passenger station was built on the new line. The site in Railway Street was then solely used for freight. Railway sidings were also provided at this site; in the builder's yard (57567, page 53 right of photograph) there is a railway truck, which is delivering materials.

Coal merchants had businesses on this site, as did the Anglo American Oil Co, all of whom had their deliveries brought in by rail. In the photograph we can see a horse-drawn carriage that may well have been one from either the Horn or White Hart hotels that met each train. In the distance can be seen the spire of St Michael's Church, and the chimney of Warner & Sons. Advertising hoardings are in evidence near the railway; Brown Brothers owned the builder's yard just below the hoarding, but they also had a timber business elsewhere in the town. The other advertisement is for Footman & Co, who had a drapery business in Bank Street - by 1929 it was being run by Ernest Larn. At the top of the road we can see the Railway Tavern, which originally opened at about the same time as the station and was then known as the London Tavern.

There was also a need for houses for professional and businessmen fairly close to the town centre. The Avenue (46722, pages 54-55) was built in the 1890s on land that was part of the Mount House estate. Mount House and its grounds are behind the fence on the left of the photo. Mount House was at this time

A GROWING TOWN

RAYNE ROAD 1907 57570

owned by Samuel Parmenter; he ran a large building firm, and he obviously had seen the development potential of the estate. People who were living in the Avenue in the early 20th century included H J Cunnington & Norman Orfeur, solicitors, James Fuller, boot and shoe manufacturer, William Lake of Lake & Elliot Ltd, and Charles Townrow, clothier and outfitter, as well as the ministers of the Congregational and Unitarian churches.

From the early part of the 20th century, houses were being built to the west of the town, along the main road to Dunmow, Rayne Road (57570, pages 56-57 and 74835, above). The houses on the right in 57570 are in the parish of Bocking and were built much earlier, possibly at the time when the Union Workhouse was built in 1837 (it was next to the last visible building on that side of the road). That last building, at the time of the photograph a pub

much larger estate developed behind Rayne Road by the Hunnable family, which became known as 'New Town'. The roads on the estate all bear the names of people or places connected with the Hunnable family. The fence on the right is that of the Union Workhouse.

The main building of the Union Workhouse (74838, pages 60-61) was built in 1837; it was the workhouse for Braintree, Bocking and the surrounding villages, with accommodation for about 400 inmates. The design of the main building is based on Jeremy Bentham's 'Panopticon', used for both prisons and workhouses at this time: from a small central building three arms radiated, with a house at the front. The Workhouse was commonly known as 'the Spike', a slang term for a place where itinerant tramps could spend the night. The building to the right of the drive was built in 1895 for this specific purpose. One of the most feared events in anyone's life was to end up 'in the house'. The regime was very strict, with complete segregation of men and women. With the creation of the National Health Service, the building became St Michael's Hospital.

called the Queen's Head, was originally a doctor's house. Notice the lack of a pavement or tarmacadam road surface - such niceties are probably 20 years away. These terraced houses were built by speculative builders, who then rented them to tenants.

As the town developed, still more houses were required; the houses that we see in 74835, above, were built on the land covered by trees in 57570, pages 56-57. These newer houses were part of a

John Wheatley MP was the man responsible for the introduction of council housing in the 1920s. As a result, there was a boom in building by local authorities; large council house estates were built in Braintree and Bocking. Apart from providing more housing for the growing town, these large-scale developments also gave much-needed employment within the building industry.

THE UNION WORKHOUSE 1923 74838

A Growing Town

A GROWING TOWN

Right: COURTAULD ROAD 1923 74837

This road runs between Coggeshall Road and Bradford Street; it replaced the old road, which ran 30 or 40 metres back from the left-hand side of this picture, when Sydney Courtauld built Bocking Place in 1885. Houses started to be built on the right-hand side of the road from the turn of the 20th century, and provided housing for the up-and-coming professional and business people.

Below: COGGESHALL ROAD 1923 74836

Continuing the development of houses along the main Dunmow to Colchester Road, these fine houses, dating from the turn of the 20th century, were also built for the growing middle class. They were known locally as 'The Villas'. Mr Leonard Alden, who ran a tailor and outfitter's business, had one of these houses.

Below Right: COUNCIL HOUSES 1923 74833

One of the early council house developments, on land at the junction of Chapel Hill and Cressing Road, is shown in this photograph. The new road to the left is Bishop's Avenue, so named because it was near where the Bishop of London's palace once stood.

A GROWING TOWN

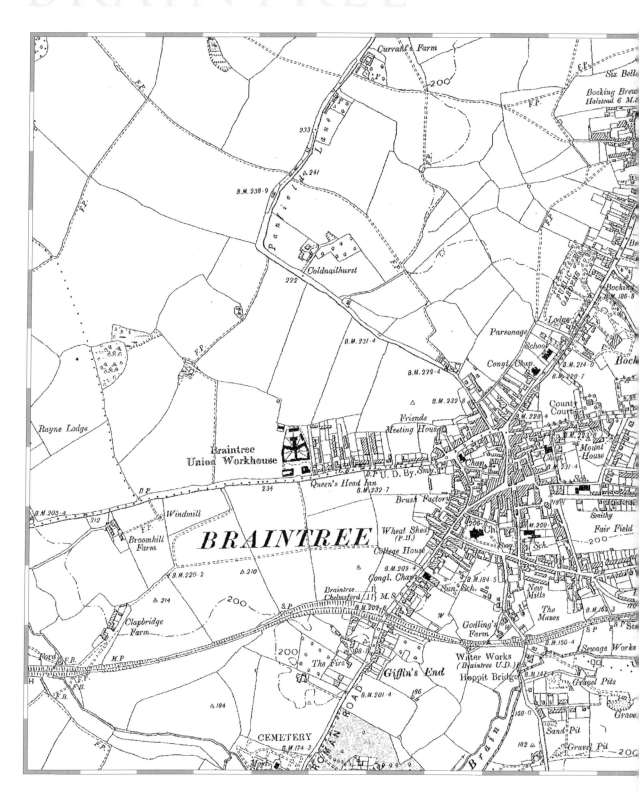

AN ORDNANCE SURVEY MAP SHOWING BRAINTREE AND SURROUNDING AREAS 1886-1896

OPEN SPACES AND RECREATION

Braintree's annual fairs provided one of the few opportunities for people to have a break from work. The fair field was on land between Manor Street and Victoria Street, behind the Town Hall. We read in the 1860 records of Samuel Courtauld & Co that workers were given time off to attend the annual May fair in Braintree and half a day off to attend a similar event in Bocking. By the 1890s these events had become fun fairs, with Mr Thurston's magnificent fairground organ as a centrepiece surrounded by the usual collection of booths and sideshows. The first films were shown at these fairs, prior to the building of the Palace cinema in about 1913. The Market Square has also been used at various times for large community events. As we move on to look at other facilities, we will notice how indebted the town is to members of the Courtauld family for such provision.

Part of Sydney Courtauld's garden was detached from the main grounds of Bocking Place by a road, and it was these 5½ acres that he gave to the people of Braintree and Bocking as a public park in 1888. Included with the gift of the park was an endowment to provide funds for its upkeep. In later years other members of the family provided additional funds. A board of Trustees is still responsible for the upkeep of the gardens. It was Mr Courtauld's idea to provide a quiet place, 'where the beauties of trees and flowers could be enjoyed in peace and safety'. Even today, visitors to the gardens can still enjoy peace and tranquillity.

THE ENTRANCE TO THE PUBLIC GARDENS 1902 48285

OPEN SPACES AND RECREATION

One of the features of the gardens is the way in which the visitor is met with different views and layouts, from open spaces to densely planted areas, or along wide pathways with narrow winding pathways off to the sides.

Not only does the park provide for individual enjoyment, but also for communal activities such as listening to the local town band on summer Sunday afternoons. In 46247, right, we have a reed-thatched bandstand, which also at times provided shelter from a sudden shower of rain. The fenced area to the left is a large open grassed area, whilst to the right are tennis courts. An essential feature in any Victorian park was a pond or lake. This pond (46246, below) was created at the far end of the park, almost hidden from view until the last minute, surrounded by formal gardens, shrubs and trees.

Another important open space is to be found at the end of the High Street near St Michael's Church where a paved and cobbled area was laid out in 1936 with a fountain centre piece.

The site was purchased by Mr G T Bartram to provide a place for a memorial to George V, which was to be provided by Mr William Julien Courtauld. The architect of the Town Hall, Mr E Vincent Harris, designed the fountain and the square. Mr John Hodges sculpted the figure of a young boy, using a member of his local scout group as a model. Sir William Llewellyn, President of the Royal Academy, opened the fountain and square on 20 July 1937. Mr W J Courtauld also gave the Dutch-style building, to the left of the square, in 1939 (see B178028, pages 74-75, left of photograph). It served as a Nurses' Home at the William Julien Courtauld Hospital in London Road. Mr W J Courtauld also gave this in 1921 as the town's war memorial for the 1914-18 war.

THE PUBLIC GARDENS 1900 46246

OPEN SPACES AND RECREATION

Above:
THE PUBLIC GARDENS
1900 46247

Left:
THE PUBLIC GARDENS
c1955 B178008

This photograph, taken nearly 70 years after the opening of the gardens, shows some of the fine specimens of trees and the formal beds of flowers.

THE PUBLIC GARDENS 1909 62120
Here we see an example of a flower-covered pergola inviting the visitor to a secluded seat amongst the shrubs.

OPEN SPACES AND RECREATION

Open Spaces and Recreation

The Public Gardens c1960 B178035

It is 60 years on from photograph 46246, page 68, and the trees and shrubs have all grown bigger. You will also note that a fountain feature has been added to the centre of the pond, and that the pond has been planted with water lilies. Behind where the people are sitting is a stream that created its own bog garden with resident water-loving creatures.

OPEN SPACES AND RECREATION

Above:

THE FOUNTAIN AND THE CHURCH c1955 B178024

Prior to 1935, all that would have been seen from in front of the church would have been the top of the church spire. In the foreground would have been a collection of dilapidated shops, and a large wooden maltings out of shot to the right. In 1935 the buildings, including the maltings, were demolished as part of a road improvement scheme.

Right:

HIGH STREET, THE FOUNTAIN c1960 B178028

74

BOCKING

BOCKING, ST PETER'S CHURCH 1900 46248

Turning up the road by the Public Gardens, we will find this church; it was built in 1896, and is known as St Peter's in the Fields because when it was originally built, it was surrounded by countryside. In 1906 a part of the parish of St Mary's, Bocking was taken to form the new parish of St Peter's. The original plans for the church included a tower and another aisle, but these were never completed.

Braintree and Bocking share a common boundary along the Dunmow to Colchester road. The railway station, until recent times, was known as Braintree & Bocking. The two townships remained separate entities until the creation of the Braintree & Bocking Urban District Council in 1934.

If we continue down Bocking End, we come to Bradford Street. This road was part of the Roman road to Suffolk, and it takes its name from the 'broad ford' which once existed over the River Blackwater. It contains some of the finest buildings in the area, some dating back to the 13th century. In 46249, page 78-79, the second house on the left with the shell porch is Georgian House, dating from about 1720; at the rear is a 16th-century house. Further down, the building with the 18th-century brick façade is Friars. Behind this façade is a much earlier 17th-century building. At one time the Maysent family, who were clothiers, occupied this house. They were the first to produce 'Long Bay' woollen cloth, which made the fortunes of many local clothiers.

B126011, pages 80-81, was taken further down the street than 46249, and shows another interesting group of buildings. The first house on the left is thought to have been a guildhall dating from 1250. The three-bay building, parts of which date back to the 15th century, was originally the Woolpack Inn, one of the many inns that served pilgrims and travellers. The last but one house is a typical 16th-century town house, whilst the one next door has an 18th-century façade hiding a 15th-century house.

Church Lane, by Braintree College, takes us to Bocking Village, more commonly known as Bocking Church Street. As the road turns towards the river, behind the trees on the left stands The Old Deanery (57574, page 79). It is now a residential home, but when this photo was taken it was the home of Dean Brownrigg. The well-kept appearance suggests that the photograph was taken shortly after alterations made in 1906.

The site was given under the will of Aetheric, the Saxon lord of the manor, in AD997. Over the years several different buildings have occupied this site. Most of this building dates from the construction of an H-plan hall house in the 1560s, although there are timbers dating back to the 13th century in the roof.

Photograph 48287, page 84, shows Bocking Church Street, and in the distance is the road to Deanery Hill. The river Blackwater flows behind the terrace of single-storey almshouses, which stand

BOCKING

BRAINTREE

on the site of almshouses provided by John Doreward in 1440. The family lived at Doreward Hall, which is across the fields behind the last cottages on the left. The building to the right was the Workmen's Hall, provided by Samuel Courtauld and Co for their workers in 1883. Their factory is to the right of the photographer, behind the hall. The hall stands on the site of an alehouse called the Kicking Dicky, and is nowadays the church hall of St Mary's church.

St Mary's (46253, page 85) stands opposite the green where the children are sitting in 48287, page 84. A church has stood on this site since Saxon times, and Aetheric was married here in AD980. Under the will of Aetheric, the manor of Bocking was gifted to Christchurch, Canterbury (later to become Canterbury Cathedral). It thus came under the jurisdiction of the Cathedral, and the priest here became a Dean and not a Vicar or Rector.

The original wooden church was replaced sometime after 1066, and was enlarged in the 13th century. The south door still retains examples of ironwork from that time. John Doreward funded the building of the lower stages of the tower in 1415. The church was rebuilt between 1490 and 1520, when the nave was heightened, a clerestory formed and the tower completed. The money for these extensive works came to a large extent from the wealth of the local woollen merchants. The view of the church today is little altered from that in the photograph.

Main Picture: BOCKING, BRADFORD STREET 1900 46249

Left: BOCKING, THE DEANERY 1907 57574

Far Right: BOCKING, THE CONVENT 1900 46252

On the opposite side of the road from 46251, pages 82-83, the ornate brick building is the Convent Chapel, built in 1899, and designed by the architect of Westminster Cathedral, Sir John Francis Bentley. This served as the Roman Catholic parish church until 1939, when the present church in the Avenue, Braintree was opened. The next-door house, known as Fulling Mill House, was the home of the Nottage family, one of Bocking's important clothiers. In the 19th century it was the home of Edith Arendrup, daughter of John Courtauld.

BOCKING

BOCKING

BOCKING

BOCKING, THE MILL 1900 46251

Here we see one of the bridges that replaced the broad ford. This bridge was replaced in 1927 with the present one so as to accommodate heavier traffic. This mill dates from 1580, but it seems likely that there was a mill here 500 years before that. Recently it has been tastefully renovated and converted into a house.

BOCKING

BOCKING

Left: BOCKING, CHURCH STREET 1902 48287

Below: BOCKING, ST MARY'S CHURCH 1900 46253

POSTSCRIPT

Braintree has changed quite considerably since the most recent photographs in this book were taken in the 1960s. Fortunately, the majority of the buildings featured in those photographs can still be seen today. The population of Braintree & Bocking has risen from 25,000 in 1961 to 40,000 by 2001. In 1964, the town was in danger of losing its railway under the Beeching axe, but the line was saved. In 1977 the line was electrified and now has a direct service to London (Liverpool Street). Unfortunately the firms of Courtauld, Warner and Lake & Elliot have closed down and Crittalls is now a shadow of its former self. In 1989 a by-pass was opened to replace the old A120 through the town and this has now become part of the new A120 to Stansted Airport and the M11. The area behind Bank Street was re-developed when the George Yard Shopping Centre opened in 1990. A first class museum was opened in the old Manor Street School in 1994 and in the autumn of 2005 a new museum housing The Warner Archive of silk fabrics and designs is opening in the former Warner's silk mills in South Street. The eastern part of the town, left derelict with the closure of the large firms, has been completely rebuilt and refurbished. In 1999 The Freeport Shopping Village was opened, with its own station on the branch line. The area now includes a 12-screen cinema, 10-pin bowling, nightclub and restaurants and plans are also in hand for a new swimming pool complex. 21st-century Braintree values its past heritage as well as embracing new and exciting opportunities.

INDEX

FRANCIS FRITH'S
TOWN&CITY
MEMORIES

BOCKING

Names of Subscribers

The following people have kindly supported this book by purchasing limited edition copies prior to publication.

Sandra and John Adlam, Braintree

In memory of Winifred Ashwell

In memory of Bearman, Bakers of Braintree

Mrs K Bennett

The D E Berry-Wright Family, Braintree

David Bird

Alice Barnett, born 2005, In Memory of Paul Boone

In Remembrance of Marge Broad, Braintree

Mr J H and Mrs J G Buttle, Braintree

The Careless Family, Braintree

Peter J Cherry, Braintree, June 2005

The Cloughton Family, Braintree

In Memory of David Collar, Finchingfield

To My Grandson Ben Collar, Braintree

In memory of Keith Collins, White Notley

The Collins Family, Braintree

Catherine Cook

Joan and Barrie Copleston

Mr Crosier, Braintree

Mr L J Crow and Mrs S E Crow, Braintree

To Mum and Dad, Braintree, on your anniversary

Mr and Mrs G R Dakin, Braintree

In memory of Mr Victor Davey

In memory of George, Mary and Lesley Hemingway
from David

In memory of Marion Dolan, Forest, VA, USA

Janet Offord and David Dow

To Dad, Philip Kirby, Love Wayne and Erin

Pauline Vines and Thelma Fisher of Braintree

In memory of Bert Foster, Braintree

Keith and Barbara French, Braintree

Stanley and Una Gill

Andrew Gladwell

Mr P L Gowers, Braintree

Malcolm and Lesley Green

The Halls Family, Braintree

The Hance Family, Braintree

Violet Hancock, née Dood, Bocking

The Hardy Family

Val and Malcolm Hasler, Black Notley

The Family of W S Gill, Furniture Dealers

Mr L D and Mrs S A Hulme, Braintree

Jim Joslin, Braintree

Mr and Mrs Dennis Joslin, Christmas 2005

Happy Birthday Nana Sullens, Love Kelly

To Bill Lincoln, from Helen

Mrs Freda Lord, commemorating your visit home
after 33 years

The Loring Family, Braintree, In memory of our
grandaughter Louise

Mr and Mrs John Mackay, Braintree

The Marshall Family, Braintree

Don and Mavourneen Moore, Braintree

Winnifred Murray, memories of Hatchet Farm

To Linda Musk, on her birthday

The Naylor Family, Braintree

In memory of Bertie and Catherine Nye

Karine and Nigel Oldacre

Peter and Pam, Braintree

The Phair Family, Bocking

In memory of Amelia Porkiss, Braintree

The Potter family, Braintree

Kathleen E Rataj, Braintree

Mr R A Sansom and P R C Readman, Braintree

In memory of Robert Richardson, Braintree

Beryl Ricketts, Braintree

Maddie, Steve and Samantha

To Margaret and John, love Samantha

The Soul Family of Braintree

In memory of Colin Stock

Jacob Oliver John Taylor, born 05/07/03

Mr Malcolm V Taylor, BEM

Paul and Margaret Taylor, Braintree

Mr Terry Thorogood on your 65th birthday

Ray Turner, Braintree

Rev Peter H West

I Wilson, Braintree and Bocking History Society

Mr H Wilson, Braintree

Margaret Wood, Braintree

The Worthington Family, Braintree

Annick A and all the Wrampling-Pounsetts

The Yeldham Family, Braintree

FRITH PRODUCTS & SERVICES

Francis Frith would doubtless be pleased to know that the pioneering publishing venture he started in 1860 still continues today. Over a hundred and forty years later, The Francis Frith Collection continues in the same innovative tradition and is now one of the foremost publishers of vintage photographs in the world. Some of the current activities include:

Interior Decoration

Today Frith's photographs can be seen framed and as giant wall murals in thousands of pubs, restaurants, hotels, banks, retail stores and other public buildings throughout the country. In every case they enhance the unique local atmosphere of the places they depict and provide reminders of gentler days in an increasingly busy and frenetic world.

Product Promotions

Frith products are used by many major companies to promote the sales of their own products or to reinforce their own history and heritage. Frith promotions have been used by Hovis bread, Courage beers, Scots Porage Oats, Colman's mustard, Cadbury's foods, Mellow Birds coffee, Dunhill pipe tobacco, Guinness, and Bulmer's Cider.

Genealogy and Family History

As the interest in family history and roots grows world-wide, more and more people are turning to Frith's photographs of Great Britain for images of the towns, villages and streets where their ancestors lived; and, of course, photographs of the churches and chapels where their ancestors were christened, married and buried are an essential part of every genealogy tree and family album.

Frith Products

All Frith photographs are available Framed or just as Mounted Prints and Posters (size 23 x 16 inches). These may be ordered from the address below. From time to time other products - Address Books, Calendars, Table Mats, etc - are available.

The Internet

Already ninety thousand Frith photographs can be viewed and purchased on the internet through the Frith websites and a myriad of partner sites.

For more detailed information on Frith companies and products, look at these sites:

www.francisfrith.co.uk
www.francisfrith.com
(for North American visitors)

See the complete list of Frith Books at:

www.francisfrith.co.uk

This web site is regularly updated with the latest list of publications from The Francis Frith Collection. If you wish to buy books relating to another part of the country that your local bookshop does not stock, you may purchase on-line.

For further information, trade, or author enquiries please contact us at the address below:
The Francis Frith Collection, Frith's Barn, Teffont, Salisbury, Wiltshire, England SP3 5QP.
Tel: +44 (0)1722 716 376 Fax: +44 (0)1722 716 881 Email: sales@francisfrith.co.uk

See Frith books on the internet at www.francisfrith.co.uk

FREE PRINT OF YOUR CHOICE

Mounted Print
Overall size 14 x 11 inches (355 x 280mm)

Choose any Frith photograph in this book.
Simply complete the Voucher opposite and return it with your remittance for £2.25 (to cover postage and handling) and we will print the photograph of your choice in SEPIA (size 11 x 8 inches) and supply it in a cream mount with a burgundy rule line (overall size 14 x 11 inches).
Please note: photographs with a reference number starting with a "Z" are not Frith photographs and cannot be supplied under this offer.
Offer valid for delivery to one UK address only.

PLUS: **Order additional Mounted Prints at HALF PRICE - £7.49 each** (normally £14.99)
If you would like to order more Frith prints from this book, possibly as gifts for friends and family, you can buy them at half price (with no additional postage and handling costs).

PLUS: **Have your Mounted Prints framed**
For an extra £14.95 per print you can have your mounted print(s) framed in an elegant polished wood and gilt moulding, overall size 16 x 13 inches (no additional postage and handling required).

IMPORTANT!

These special prices are only available if you use this form to order. You must use the ORIGINAL VOUCHER on this page (no copies permitted). We can only despatch to one UK address. This offer cannot be combined with any other offer.

Send completed Voucher form to:
The Francis Frith Collection, Frith's Barn, Teffont, Salisbury, Wiltshire SP3 5QP

CHOOSE A PHOTOGRAPH FROM THIS BOOK

Voucher for *FREE* and Reduced Price Frith Prints

Please do not photocopy this voucher. Only the original is valid, so please fill it in, cut it out and return it to us with your order.

Picture ref no	Page no	Qty	Mounted @ £7.49	Framed + £14.95	Total Cost £
		1	Free of charge*	£	£
			£7.49	£	£
			£7.49	£	£
			£7.49	£	£
			£7.49	£	£
			£7.49	£	£

Please allow 28 days for delivery. Offer available to one UK address only

* Post & handling	£2.25
Total Order Cost	£

Title of this book . . . .

I enclose a cheque/postal order for £ . . . .
made payable to 'The Francis Frith Collection'

OR please debit my Mastercard / Visa / Maestro / Amex card, details below

Card Number

Issue No (Maestro only)   Valid from (Maestro)

Expires   Signature

Name Mr/Mrs/Ms . . . .
Address . . . .
. . . .
. . . .
. . . . Postcode . . . .
Daytime Tel No . . . .
Email . . . .

ISBN 1-85937-987-7   Valid to 31/12/08

Can you help us with information about any of the Frith photographs in this book?

We are gradually compiling an historical record for each of the photographs in the Frith archive. It is always fascinating to find out the names of the people shown in the pictures, as well as insights into the shops, buildings and other features depicted.

If you recognize anyone in the photographs in this book, or if you have information not already included in the author's caption, do let us know. We would love to hear from you, and will try to publish it in future books or articles.

Our production team

Frith books are produced by a small dedicated team at offices in the converted Grade II listed 18th-century barn at Teffont near Salisbury, illustrated above. Most have worked with the Frith Collection for many years. All have in common one quality: they have a passion for the Frith Collection. The team is constantly expanding, but currently includes:

Paul Baron, Jason Buck, John Buck, Ruth Butler, Heather Crisp, David Davies, Louis du Mont, Isobel Hall, Lucy Hart, Julian Hight, Peter Horne, James Kinnear, Karen Kinnear, Tina Leary, Stuart Login, Sue Molloy, Sarah Roberts, Kate Rotondetto, Dean Scource, Eliza Sackett, Terence Sackett, Sandra Sampson, Adrian Sanders, Sandra Sanger, Julia Skinner, Miles Smith, Lewis Taylor, Shelley Tolcher, Lorraine Tuck, Miranda Tunnicliffe, David Turner and Ricky Williams.